Where Fish Go in Winter
And Other Great Mysteries

BY **Amy Goldman Koss**

ILLUSTRATED BY **Laura J. Bryant**

PUFFIN BOOKS

To Uncle Hy—A.G.K.
To Paco—L.J.B.

PUFFIN BOOKS
Published by the Penguin Group
Penguin Putnam Books for Young Readers,
345 Hudson Street, New York, New York 10014, U.S.A.
Penguin Books Ltd, 80 Strand, London WC2R ORL, England
Penguin Books Australia Ltd, Ringwood, Victoria, Australia
Penguin Books Canada Ltd, 10 Alcorn Avenue, Toronto, Ontario, Canada M4V 3B2
Penguin Books (N.Z.) Ltd, 182-190 Wairau Road, Auckland 10, New Zealand

Penguin Books Ltd, Registered Offices: Harmondsworth, Middlesex, England

First published in the United States of America by Price Stern Sloan, Inc., 1987
Published with new illustrations by Puffin Books,
a division of Penguin Putnam Books for Young Readers, 2002
Simultaneously published in hard cover by Dial Books for Young Readers

The original PSS edition was published with the subtitle
"And Answers to Other Great Mysteries"

1   3   5   7   9   10   8   6   4   2

Text copyright © Amy Goldman Koss, 1987
Illustrations copyright © Laura J. Bryant, 2002
All rights reserved

LIBRARY OF CONGRESS CATALOGING-IN-PUBLICATION DATA
Koss, Amy Goldman, date.
Where fish go in winter : and other great mysteries / by Amy GoldmanKoss;
illustrated by Laura J. Bryant.
p.   cm.—(Puffin easy-to-read. Level 3)
Summary: A collection of poems that answer such questions as
"Where do fish go in winter?" and "Why does popcorn pop?"
ISBN 0-8037-2704-6 (hardcover) - ISBN 0-14-230038-1 (pbk.)
1. Science—Miscellanea—Juvenile literature. [1. Science—Miscellanea. 2.
Questions and answers.] I. Bryant, Laura, ill. II. Title. III. Series.
Q163 .K67 2002
500—dc21
2001054820

Printed in Hong Kong

Reading Level 3.2

DEAR FRIENDS,
My head was so packed full of questions to ask,
That listing them all was quite a big task.
I called on biologists, botanists, too,
Doctors, and teachers, and folks at the zoo.

My thanks to the experts, so patient and kind.
With their friendly help I was able to find
The answers I'm sharing with you in this book.
I hope that you like it. So please take a look!

Sincerely,

Where do fish go in winter?

When lakes turn to ice
And are covered with snow,
What becomes of the fish
Who are living below?

It's not so exciting
Down under the ice,
But fish find it restful
And really quite nice.

It's dark and it's cold,
But the water's not frozen.
In fact, it's just perfect
For fish to repose in.

They breathe very little.
Their swimming gets slower.
Each fish makes his heart rate
Go lower and lower.

And except for occasional
Lake bottom treats,
The whole winter long
The fish hardly eats.

Why does popcorn pop?

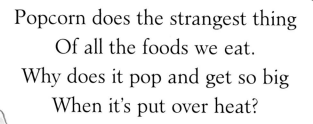

Popcorn does the strangest thing
Of all the foods we eat.
Why does it pop and get so big
When it's put over heat?

Popcorn kernels have a shell
That keeps their moisture in.
The kernel's shell is fairly tough,
But also very thin.

When you heat the kernels up,
The moisture turns to steam.
And if you make them hotter still,
The pressure gets extreme.

The steam inside the shell expands,
The kernel overloads,
'Til it's as full as it can be,
And—*POP!*— the corn explodes!

6

How do birds fly?

If I had wings
Could I then fly,
And swoop and soar
Across the sky?

To fly, I'd need
Much more than wings,
'Cause wings are just
The start of things.

Some birds have wings
That are too small.
So ostriches
Can't fly at all!

A flying bird's
Proportioned right,
To make her swift
And strong and light.

Her beak weighs less
Than teeth and jaws.
Her bones are hollow,
Head to claws.

With lungs and heart
Big for her size,
She hardly tires
When she flies.

And feathers are
The perfect touch.
They keep her warm,
But don't weigh much.

Do islands float?

Does an island
Bob and float
Upon the ocean
Like a boat?

Islands are the
Part we see
Of mountains
Underneath the sea.

They're as solid
And as still
As any other
Ridge or hill.

They do not move
Despite the motion
Of the heaving,
Rocking ocean.

Why do snakes shed their skins?

Elephants don't shed their skins,
Nor pigs nor goats nor crows.
So why do snakes take off their skins
Like people take off clothes?

Snake skin doesn't stretch too much,
And snake skin doesn't grow.
So as the snake gets bigger,
He has no place else to go.

He simply has no other choice,
Except to shed his skin.
He slides it off in one long piece,
Beginning with his chin.

Before he's through, he even sheds
The clear skin from his eyes.
And then he wears a brand-new skin
That's in a larger size!

What do clouds feel like?

Would clouds feel fluffy,
Soft, and grand
If I could touch them
With my hand?

To clutch a cloud
Inside your fist
Would be like holding
Morning mist.

Clouds are not
The way they seem.
They weigh no more
Than fog or steam.

They're made of tiny
Water drops,
So light they float
Above rooftops.

15

How do cats purr?

A dog knows how to wag her tail,
But only kitties purr.
How do they make that purring sound,
So deep inside their fur?

Their belly muscles flutter
When people pet their coats.
The flutters send small puffs of air
Up to the kitties' throats.

There the tiny puffs become
The purring sound so sweet.
Hold a happy kitty close
And feel the rapid beat.

Bigger cats, like tigers, purr.
Cheetahs do it, too.
They purr just like a kitty does.
I think that's neat, don't you?

Why do leaves change colors?

The oak tree always lets me know
When autumn has begun.
But why do summer's dark green leaves
Change colors one by one?

It's chlorophyll that feeds the tree
And makes the leaves look green.
But underneath are chemicals
In hues that can't be seen.

When summertime has gone away,
And days grow short and cold,
The chlorophyll then fades away,
Revealing flecks of gold.

When all the chlorophyll is gone,
Instead of green, we see
The lovely yellow, orange, and red,
In bright leaves on the tree!

What is the sound in a seashell?

Inside the shell there is a sound,
Mysterious to me.
How is it that the seashell can
Sound so much like the sea?

A seashell held up to your ear
Will block out background sound.
So if you used a jar instead,
The same sound would be found.

Air molecules that bounce around
Are half of what you hear.
And half the sound is your own blood
That's rushing through your ear!

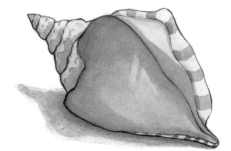

What is the Man in the Moon?

What puts the face
On the Man in the Moon?
Is it the shadows
Of crater and dune?

No mountain or crater
Is so high or low
That seen from our planet
Its shadow would show.

The face isn't shadows,
The scientists find,
But rocks the moon's made of
And how they combine.

Some rocks absorb light,
And others reflect it—
That changes the way
That our eyes detect it.

So sunlight's reflection
Off each different place
Makes light and dark patches,
Which form the moon's face.

Do turtles leave their shells?

The turtle's shell is cumbersome
And makes his movements slow.
Why doesn't he just take it off?
That's what I'd like to know.

Between his backbone and his shell
There is a strong connection.
It suits him well, he likes to have
His own built-in protection.

For if he tried to leave his shell,
He'd have to leave his bones as well.
So turtles really do not mind
That they can't leave their shells behind.

Do spiders stick
to their own webs?

The spider weaves a sticky web
To capture bugs to eat.
What keeps the spider's sticky web
From sticking to her feet?

Spiderwebs are very tricky
Because not all the strands are sticky.
Unlike the passing hapless fly,
The spider knows which strands are dry.

But if by accident she stands
On any of the sticky strands,
She still would not get stuck, you see—
Her oily body slides off free.

Why do onions make us cry?

Tomatoes do not make us cry,
But onions surely do.
Why do onions bring on tears
And make us go "boo hoo"?

When we cut an onion up,
We break apart its cells.
Inside the cell is onion oil,
Which really, really smells!

The oil turns to vapors
That sting our nose and eyes.
To wash away the stinging stuff
The eye makes tears and cries!

How do seeds know which way is up?

It's dark underground
Where sunlight can't go,
So how does a seed
Know which way to grow?

The root is the first
To grow from the seed—
Down into the darkness
It digs at full speed.

Gravity sensors
Within each young root
Teach it to follow
A straight downward route.

And once this young root
Has taken the lead,
A tender green shoot
Sprouts out of the seed.

The shoot only knows
That its life's pursuit
Means heading the opposite
Way of the root.

Since shoots need the sunlight
To live and to grow,
They force themselves upward
Through dark dirt below.

The roots need the water
And the shoots need the light.
Each goes its own way,
And that works out just right!

Thanks to
Barry and My Freen